I0845745

Tech and Aging:
Enhancing Lives Through Assistive Technologies

By

Melodee K. Nickens

Tech and Aging:
Enhancing Lives Through Assistive Technologies

Copyright © by **Melodee K. Nickens** 2023. All rights reserved. Before this document is duplicated or reproduced in any manner, the publisher's consent must be gained. Therefore, the contents within can neither be stored electronically, transferred, nor kept in a database. Neither in Part nor full can the document be copied, scanned, faxed, or retained without approval from the publisher or creator.

TABLE OF CONTENTS

CHAPTER I
Introduction

A. The Intersection of Technology and Aging

In recent decades, the world has witnessed remarkable advancements in technology that have transformed every aspect of our lives. From communication to transportation, and from healthcare to entertainment, technology has become an inseparable part of the modern human experience. Amidst this digital revolution, one of the most profound societal shifts has been the aging of the population.

As the global population continues to age, societies are facing unprecedented challenges in providing adequate care and support for the elderly. According to the World Health Organization, the number of people aged 60 years and older is expected to double by 2050, reaching over two billion. This demographic shift not only demands a reevaluation of healthcare systems and social support structures but also presents an opportunity to harness the potential of technology to enhance the lives of older adults.

The intersection of technology and aging brings forth a plethora of possibilities, as assistive technologies emerge as powerful tools to address the unique needs of the elderly. These technologies are designed to assist individuals in maintaining independence, improving health outcomes, and enabling active engagement with the world around them. By bridging the gap between age-related limitations and everyday tasks, assistive technologies have the potential to revolutionize the aging experience.

In this book, "Tech and Aging: Enhancing Lives Through Assistive Technologies," we delve into the dynamic relationship between technology and aging, exploring how innovative solutions can positively impact the lives of seniors. We aim to provide a comprehensive understanding of the current landscape of assistive technologies, their applications, and the challenges and opportunities they present.

As we embark on this journey, we recognize the multifaceted nature of aging and the diverse experiences of older individuals. The aging process is not uniform; it varies from person to person, influenced by genetics, lifestyle, and environmental factors. Likewise, technology is not a one-size-fits-all solution, necessitating a thoughtful and personalized approach to incorporating assistive technologies into the lives of seniors.

Throughout this book, we will explore various categories of assistive technologies, ranging from mobility assistance devices and cognitive support tools to sensory aids and health monitoring solutions. We will highlight real-life case studies that demonstrate the transformative impact of these technologies on individuals' lives, enriching their experiences and fostering independence.

Moreover, we will address the challenges and barriers that exist in the integration of technology into aging populations. Accessibility, usability, privacy, and ethical concerns are crucial aspects that demand thoughtful consideration to ensure that these technologies benefit everyone, leaving no one behind.

We also recognize the invaluable role played by caregivers and healthcare professionals in the lives of seniors. The book will explore how technology can empower caregivers, enhance their abilities, and promote collaborative care models that optimize the support provided to the elderly.

In conclusion, "Tech and Aging: Enhancing Lives Through Assistive Technologies" is a comprehensive exploration of the synergies between technology and aging. As we unravel the potential of assistive technologies, we hope to inspire readers to embrace these innovations and actively contribute to a future where aging is met with dignity, independence, and enriched experiences. Join us as we embark on this transformative journey to create a world where technology uplifts the lives of individuals, regardless of their age or abilities.

B. Importance of Assistive Technologies

In the rapidly evolving landscape of technology, one area that holds immense significance is the development and implementation of assistive technologies. As the global population continues to age, the need for these innovative solutions becomes more pressing than ever before. "Tech and Aging: Enhancing Lives Through Assistive Technologies" explores the vital role these technologies play in improving the quality of life for older adults and addressing the challenges associated with aging.

Assistive technologies refer to a wide range of tools, devices, and systems that are designed to aid individuals with various disabilities and limitations, empowering them to perform tasks, enhance their capabilities, and participate more actively in daily life. While these technologies have been beneficial to individuals with disabilities across all age groups, their impact on the aging population is particularly noteworthy.

Aging is a natural and inevitable part of life, and as individuals grow older, they may encounter physical, sensory, cognitive, and mobility changes that can pose significant challenges to their independence and well-being. Simple activities like getting dressed, preparing meals, or even communicating with loved ones can become difficult without the right support. This is where assistive technologies step in to bridge the gap and offer solutions that cater to the unique needs of older adults.

One of the primary benefits of assistive technologies is the preservation of independence. Aging individuals often value their autonomy and wish to remain in their homes and communities for as long as possible. Assistive technologies enable them to do just that by facilitating tasks that might otherwise require assistance. For example, mobility assistance devices such as walking aids or motorized scooters can help seniors maintain their mobility and freedom to move around independently.

Moreover, assistive technologies contribute to improved health outcomes for aging individuals. From health monitoring devices that track vital signs to reminder systems for medication management, these technologies can help seniors manage chronic conditions and promote proactive healthcare practices. Timely intervention and better disease management can prevent complications and hospitalizations, leading to a higher quality of life.

Another vital aspect of assistive technologies is their role in fostering social connectivity and combating isolation. Social isolation is a prevalent issue among older adults, and it can have adverse effects on mental health and well-being. Communication tools, video conferencing platforms, and virtual reality applications allow seniors to stay connected with family and friends, participate in social activities, and engage in virtual communities, reducing feelings of loneliness and promoting a sense of belonging.

Furthermore, by enhancing accessibility and usability, assistive technologies ensure that products and services are inclusive and equitable for individuals of all ages and abilities. This approach not only benefits older adults but also creates a more inclusive society, where diversity is celebrated, and everyone can actively participate in various aspects of life.

In "Tech and Aging: Enhancing Lives Through Assistive Technologies," we delve into the transformative power of these innovations, exploring real-life case studies and success stories that exemplify the positive impact they have had on seniors' lives. We also acknowledge the challenges and barriers that must be addressed to ensure these technologies reach those who need them the most and that they are deployed responsibly and ethically.

As we progress through the book, we invite readers to join us in recognizing the significance of assistive technologies in shaping the future of aging. By understanding their potential and advocating for their integration into society, we can collectively work towards a world where technology empowers older adults, enhances their independence, and enables them to lead fulfilling lives with dignity and respect.

C. Overview of the Book's Scope

Welcome to "Tech and Aging: Enhancing Lives Through Assistive Technologies," a comprehensive exploration of the dynamic relationship between technology and the aging population. In this book, we embark on a journey to uncover the transformative potential of assistive technologies and their role in improving the lives of older adults.

Part A of our introduction highlighted the intersection of technology and aging, emphasizing the demographic trends that have led to a rapidly aging global population. With the number of seniors projected to double in the coming decades, it is crucial to address the unique challenges and opportunities that this demographic shift presents. This brings us to Part B of the introduction – the importance of assistive technologies.

At its core, this book aims to shed light on the significance of assistive technologies in enhancing the lives of aging individuals. We recognize that aging is a diverse and multifaceted process, and each person's experience is unique. Assistive technologies serve as valuable tools to support individuals as they age, regardless of their physical, cognitive, or sensory abilities. From mobility assistance devices that provide the freedom to move around independently to cognitive support technologies that bolster memory and cognitive functions, these innovations play a vital role in addressing the specific needs of older adults.

One of the primary reasons assistive technologies are of utmost importance is their ability to preserve and promote independence among seniors. Aging individuals often strive to maintain their autonomy and continue to participate actively in their daily lives. Assistive technologies empower them to achieve these goals, enabling them to accomplish tasks and engage in activities that might otherwise be challenging. By fostering independence, these technologies not only improve the overall well-being of seniors but also relieve the burden on caregivers and healthcare systems.

The significance of assistive technologies extends to healthcare and wellness outcomes as well. Through health monitoring and telehealth solutions, seniors can actively manage their health conditions, adhere to treatment plans, and detect potential issues at an early stage. This proactive approach to healthcare can lead to better disease management, reduced hospitalizations, and ultimately, an improved quality of life.

Beyond physical well-being, assistive technologies also play a critical role in addressing the social and emotional needs of older adults. With social isolation being a prevalent issue among seniors, communication tools and virtual platforms enable them to connect with loved ones, engage in social activities, and participate in virtual communities. These technologies combat feelings of loneliness, promote social interaction, and foster a sense of belonging.

In this book, we aim to provide readers with a comprehensive understanding of the various types of assistive technologies available for aging individuals. We delve into mobility assistance devices, cognitive support technologies, sensory aids, communication tools, and health monitoring solutions. Each chapter explores the applications and benefits of these technologies, supported by real-life case studies and testimonials from individuals who have experienced their positive impact firsthand.

We also acknowledge the challenges and barriers that must be addressed to ensure equitable access to these technologies for all older adults. Issues of accessibility, usability, privacy, and ethical considerations are vital aspects that demand thoughtful and responsible implementation.

In conclusion, "Tech and Aging: Enhancing Lives Through Assistive Technologies" strives to be a valuable resource for readers seeking to understand the critical role of technology in improving the aging experience. By recognizing the importance of assistive technologies and advocating for their widespread integration, we can work together to create a more inclusive, supportive, and empowering environment for older adults worldwide. Join us as we explore the transformative power of technology and its potential to enrich the lives of aging individuals, empowering them to age with grace and dignity.

CHAPTER II
Understanding Aging and Its Challenges

A. Demographic Trends and Aging Population

The demographic landscape of the world is undergoing a profound transformation as a result of increasing life expectancy and declining birth rates. These shifts have led to a significant increase in the proportion of older adults in the global population. As we explore the relationship between technology and aging, it is essential to understand the demographic trends and the implications of an aging population.

Demographic trends reveal a substantial increase in the number of people aged 60 years and older, a phenomenon commonly referred to as population aging. This demographic shift is largely attributed to advancements in healthcare, improved living conditions, and better access to nutrition and medical services, all of which have contributed to longer lifespans. Additionally, declining birth rates in many countries have led to a reduction in the number of younger individuals relative to older age groups, further accentuating the aging trend.

According to data from the United Nations, the number of people aged 60 and above is growing at an unprecedented rate, with projections indicating a continued upward trajectory. This global phenomenon has far-reaching implications for societies, economies, and public policies. Countries around the world are grappling with the challenges and opportunities presented by this demographic shift.

One of the most immediate challenges posed by population aging is the strain on healthcare systems. With an increasing number of older adults requiring medical care and long-term support, healthcare providers and resources are under pressure to meet the growing demand. Chronic conditions and age-related ailments become more prevalent in older age groups, necessitating specialized care and attention.

Economic implications of an aging population are significant as well. As the proportion of working-age individuals decreases, the potential workforce shrinks, leading to concerns about labor shortages and productivity. The burden on pension and social security systems also increases as more individuals rely on retirement benefits. Governments and policymakers face the task of ensuring the sustainability of social welfare programs while fostering economic growth.

In addition to healthcare and economic concerns, population aging also brings social and cultural changes. Traditional family structures, where multiple generations lived under one roof, are becoming less common. This shift can affect the social support networks available to older adults, potentially leading to issues of social isolation and loneliness.

However, amid these challenges, there are also opportunities presented by an aging population. Older adults possess a wealth of knowledge, experience, and skills that can be harnessed to contribute to society in various ways. Leveraging the talents of older adults can lead to intergenerational collaboration and the exchange of wisdom between generations.

As we delve into the intersection of technology and aging, it becomes apparent that assistive technologies have a crucial role to play in addressing the challenges associated with an aging population. These technologies have the potential to alleviate the burden on healthcare systems, enhance independence and well-being, and foster social connectivity among seniors.

In "Tech and Aging: Enhancing Lives Through Assistive Technologies," we seek to explore these possibilities and shed light on the ways technology can positively impact the lives of older adults. By understanding the demographic trends and the realities of aging, we can lay the foundation for creating a more inclusive, supportive, and age-friendly society that embraces the potential of technology to enrich the lives of all individuals, regardless of their age.

B. Physical and Cognitive Changes in Aging

Aging is a complex and natural process that brings about a myriad of physical and cognitive changes in individuals.

As we explore the intersection of technology and aging, it is essential to understand these changes and their implications on the well-being and functioning of older adults.

Physical Changes: As people age, they experience a range of physical changes that impact their overall health and mobility. Some of the common physical changes associated with aging include:

a. Muscle Mass and Strength: With age, there is a gradual loss of muscle mass and a decline in muscle strength, known as sarcopenia. This can lead to reduced mobility, balance issues, and an increased risk of falls.

b. Bone Density: Bone density tends to decrease as individuals age, making older adults more susceptible to fractures and osteoporosis.

c. Joint Health: The cartilage in joints may wear down over time, leading to conditions such as arthritis, which can cause pain and limited range of motion.

d. Vision and Hearing: Aging often results in changes to vision and hearing. Visual acuity may decrease, and conditions like cataracts and age-related macular degeneration can impair vision. Hearing loss, known as presbycusis, is also common in older adults.

e. Cardiovascular Health: The cardiovascular system undergoes changes with age, leading to reduced heart efficiency and increased risk of heart-related conditions.

f. Digestive System: Aging can affect the digestive system, leading to issues such as decreased appetite, slower digestion, and constipation.

Cognitive Changes: Cognitive changes are another crucial aspect of aging that can influence memory, attention, and decision-making abilities. While cognitive aging varies from person to person, some common changes include:

a. Memory: Older adults may experience difficulties with short-term memory and processing speed. Long-term memory tends to remain relatively stable.

b. Attention and Focus: Aging can impact attention span and the ability to focus on complex tasks for prolonged periods.

c. Problem-Solving and Decision Making: Older adults may take longer to make decisions and find it challenging to solve complex problems compared to younger individuals.

d. Language and Communication: Language skills, such as word retrieval and verbal fluency, may decline with age.

e. Executive Functions: Executive functions, which involve planning, organizing, and multitasking, may be affected in some individuals.

It is essential to note that while these physical and cognitive changes are common in aging, they do not necessarily result in significant impairments for every individual. Healthy lifestyle choices, regular exercise, proper nutrition, and mental stimulation can play a crucial role in maintaining cognitive and physical well-being as people age.

In the context of technology and aging, understanding these changes is vital in designing assistive technologies that cater to the specific needs of older adults. By considering the physical and cognitive capabilities and limitations, developers can create user-friendly and accessible solutions that empower seniors to remain independent, engaged, and active members of society.

In the upcoming chapters of "Tech and Aging: Enhancing Lives Through Assistive Technologies," we will delve deeper into the various types of assistive technologies that address the challenges posed by these physical and cognitive changes. From mobility aids and health monitoring devices to cognitive support tools, we will explore how technology can be harnessed to enhance the lives of older adults and promote healthy aging. Join us on this enlightening journey as we uncover the power of technology in shaping the future of aging.

C. Social and Emotional Impact of Aging

Aging is not merely a biological process; it is also deeply intertwined with social and emotional aspects of an individual's life. As people grow older, they undergo significant changes in their social circles, emotional well-being, and overall quality of life. Exploring the social and emotional impact of aging is essential to understanding the holistic experience of older adults and addressing the challenges they may encounter.

Social Impact of Aging:

a. Changes in Social Circles: As individuals age, they may experience changes in their social networks. Retirement, relocation, and the passing of friends and family members can lead to a reduction in social interactions, potentially leading to feelings of isolation and loneliness.

b. Role Transitions: Aging often involves significant role transitions, such as becoming a grandparent or retiring from a long-standing career. These transitions can alter an individual's sense of identity and purpose, requiring adaptation to new roles and responsibilities.

c. Social Support: The availability of social support is crucial in later life. Older adults who have strong social support systems tend to experience better mental and physical health, while those lacking support may face increased vulnerability and stress.

d. Intergenerational Relationships: Aging individuals often have opportunities to foster intergenerational relationships with younger family members or through community activities. These connections can be enriching and mutually beneficial, offering valuable perspectives to both age groups.

e. Community Engagement: Active community engagement and participation in social activities can positively impact the overall well-being of older adults. Involvement in clubs, volunteer work, or cultural events can foster a sense of belonging and purpose.

Emotional Impact of Aging:

a. Coping with Loss: As individuals age, they may face multiple losses, including the loss of loved ones, physical abilities, and independence. Coping with these losses can be emotionally challenging and may require support and resilience.

b. Psychological Well-being: Mental health is a significant aspect of aging. Older adults may experience a range of emotions, from contentment and fulfillment to feelings of sadness or anxiety. Promoting positive mental health and addressing mental health issues are essential components of aging well.

c. Resilience and Adaptability: Aging individuals demonstrate varying levels of resilience and adaptability to life's changes and challenges. Building resilience can help older adults navigate life transitions and maintain a positive outlook on aging.

d. Life Satisfaction: Life satisfaction in later years is influenced by various factors, including health, relationships, and self-perception. Positive experiences and a sense of purpose contribute to higher life satisfaction.

e. Facing Stigma: Ageism and stereotypes surrounding aging can have a negative impact on older adults' emotional well-being. Addressing age-related stigma is crucial to promoting a positive and inclusive view of aging.

Understanding the social and emotional impact of aging is essential for developing effective support systems and interventions that cater to the unique needs of older adults. In the context of technology and aging, innovative assistive technologies can play a significant role in addressing social isolation, fostering social connectivity, and promoting emotional well-being.

In the subsequent chapters of "Tech and Aging: Enhancing Lives Through Assistive Technologies," we will explore how technology can be leveraged to address the social and emotional challenges faced by older adults. From virtual communication platforms to interactive social engagement solutions, we will investigate how technology can enhance the social fabric and emotional resilience of aging individuals. By embracing technology with a focus on human-centered design, we can create a more compassionate and supportive environment for older adults, empowering them to age with dignity, fulfillment, and a sense of belonging in the ever-evolving world.

CHAPTER III
The Evolution of Assistive Technologies

A. Historical Overview of Assistive Devices

The history of assistive technologies is a testament to human ingenuity and compassion, dating back to ancient civilizations. Throughout the ages, individuals have sought innovative solutions to support those with disabilities and age-related limitations, paving the way for the diverse array of assistive devices we have today.

Ancient civilizations, such as the Egyptians and Greeks, were among the first to develop rudimentary assistive devices. Historical records indicate the use of prosthetic limbs made from wood and leather to aid individuals with limb loss or impairment. These early prosthetics aimed to restore mobility and functionality, providing a glimpse into the human desire to overcome physical challenges.

In the Middle Ages, advancements in metallurgy led to more sophisticated prosthetic limbs made from iron and copper. However, access to such devices was limited, and assistive technologies remained largely confined to local artisans and skilled craftsmen.

The Renaissance period saw a resurgence of interest in human anatomy and the study of disabilities. The renowned artist and inventor Leonardo da Vinci conceptualized designs for innovative prosthetic limbs, showcasing his visionary approach to assistive technologies. Although many of his inventions remained theoretical, they laid the groundwork for future innovations.

The 19th and early 20th centuries marked a turning point in the development of assistive technologies. The Industrial Revolution facilitated mass production, making prosthetic limbs and other assistive devices more accessible to a broader population. The advent of new materials, such as vulcanized rubber and lightweight metals, further improved the functionality and comfort of assistive devices.

World War I and World War II brought a surge in demand for assistive technologies due to the large number of veterans with disabilities. These conflicts stimulated significant advancements in prosthetics, mobility aids, and sensory devices. Innovations like the "Jaipur foot" in India, a low-cost and highly functional prosthetic, exemplified the potential of collaborative efforts in the field of assistive technologies.

The latter half of the 20th century witnessed a rapid expansion in assistive technologies driven by technological breakthroughs and the rise of electronic and digital advancements. Electronic hearing aids, powered wheelchairs, and communication devices for individuals with speech impairments revolutionized the lives of those with disabilities.

With the advent of the digital age, assistive technologies have become more sophisticated, adaptable, and personalized. Computers and smart devices have opened new possibilities for individuals with disabilities, enabling them to access information, communicate, and interact with the world in previously unimaginable ways.

Today, assistive technologies encompass a vast range of devices and solutions, from wearable health monitors and exoskeletons that enhance mobility to voice-activated smart home systems that promote independence. Artificial intelligence and machine learning have further accelerated the development of assistive technologies, enabling personalized and context-aware support for individuals with diverse needs.

As we explore the historical evolution of assistive devices in "Tech and Aging: Enhancing Lives Through Assistive Technologies," we pay homage to the pioneers who paved the way for these innovations. We also acknowledge the continuous efforts of researchers, engineers, and caregivers who work tirelessly to push the boundaries of what is possible in the realm of assistive technologies. By understanding the historical context, we gain a deeper appreciation for the transformative power of these technologies and the potential they hold to create a more inclusive and compassionate society.

B. Technological Advancements in Recent Years

In recent years, the world has witnessed remarkable technological advancements that have significantly transformed the landscape of assistive technologies. These innovations have ushered in a new era of possibilities, empowering individuals with disabilities and older adults to lead more independent, fulfilling lives. The rapid convergence of technology and aging has given rise to a plethora of cutting-edge solutions, revolutionizing the field of assistive technologies.

One of the most notable technological advancements in recent years is the widespread adoption of wearable devices. These compact, sensor-packed gadgets can be worn on the body or integrated into clothing and accessories. Wearable health monitors have become increasingly popular, allowing individuals to track vital signs, monitor physical activity, and even detect potential health issues in real-time. For seniors, such devices offer valuable insights into their well-being, encouraging proactive health management and early intervention.

The advent of smartphones and smart devices has played a pivotal role in enhancing the accessibility and usability of assistive technologies. Mobile applications and voice-activated assistants have become powerful tools for older adults and individuals with disabilities. These devices can perform tasks such as setting reminders, managing appointments, and providing voice-controlled navigation, significantly improving convenience and quality of life.

Artificial intelligence (AI) and machine learning have emerged as game-changers in the field of assistive technologies. AI-powered solutions can adapt and learn from user interactions, providing personalized support based on individual needs and preferences. For example, AI-based language processing technologies enable more natural and accurate communication for individuals with speech impairments, while machine learning algorithms can anticipate user requirements, enhancing user experience.

Robotics has also witnessed significant advancements in recent years, offering promising applications in the domain of assistive technologies. Robots can provide physical assistance and support to individuals with mobility challenges, helping with tasks like standing, walking, and picking up objects. Social robots have been developed to engage and interact with older adults, providing companionship and reducing feelings of loneliness.

Virtual reality (VR) and augmented reality (AR) have opened up new possibilities for training, rehabilitation, and cognitive support. VR-based simulations are used to help individuals regain motor skills after injuries or strokes, while AR solutions can enhance visual and auditory experiences for those with sensory impairments.

Telehealth and remote monitoring technologies have become indispensable in the face of global challenges like the COVID-19 pandemic. These technologies enable healthcare providers to deliver medical services remotely, ensuring continuous care for aging individuals and those with mobility limitations.

The integration of assistive technologies with the Internet of Things (IoT) has further expanded the capabilities of these devices. IoT-enabled devices can communicate with each other and share data, creating interconnected ecosystems that improve the efficiency and effectiveness of assistive technologies.

In "Tech and Aging: Enhancing Lives Through Assistive Technologies," we explore these technological advancements and their transformative impact on the aging experience. By embracing innovation and human-centered design, we can harness the full potential of these technologies to create a more inclusive and accessible future for older adults and individuals with disabilities. The continuous evolution of assistive technologies inspires hope for a world where age and ability are no longer barriers to leading fulfilling and empowered lives.

C. Current State of Assistive Technologies

The current state of assistive technologies is marked by unprecedented innovation and widespread accessibility. Advancements in various fields, including electronics, software development, artificial intelligence, and robotics, have converged to create a diverse and comprehensive range of assistive devices and solutions. These technologies are transforming the lives of individuals with disabilities and older adults, enabling them to overcome challenges, enhance their independence, and engage more actively in society.

One of the most significant developments in the current state of assistive technologies is the focus on user-centered design. Manufacturers and developers are increasingly prioritizing the needs and preferences of end-users, ensuring that assistive devices are intuitive, customizable, and adaptable. Human-computer interaction research and usability studies have played a vital role in refining user interfaces and optimizing the overall user experience.

The prevalence of smartphones and smart devices has opened up a new realm of possibilities for assistive technologies. These devices are equipped with numerous sensors and capabilities, making them ideal platforms for hosting assistive applications and services. Mobile apps offer a wide range of functions, from communication and navigation aids to cognitive support and health monitoring tools. Moreover, app stores now house an ever-expanding collection of assistive apps, providing users with a vast array of choices to cater to their specific needs.

Artificial intelligence has become an integral part of many assistive technologies, enabling personalized and context-aware support. AI-powered speech recognition and natural language processing technologies facilitate more natural communication for individuals with speech impairments. Machine learning algorithms are utilized in predictive text entry, auto-correction, and adaptive interfaces, tailoring the user experience to individual abilities and preferences.

The current state of robotics in assistive technologies is witnessing significant advancements. Robotic exoskeletons and wearable devices can augment the strength and mobility of individuals with physical disabilities, providing support during walking and rehabilitation. Social robots are being developed to engage and interact with older adults, providing companionship and assisting with daily tasks.

Sensory assistive technologies have also made remarkable progress, especially in the field of visual and auditory support. Advanced hearing aids and cochlear implants offer improved sound processing and enhanced hearing experiences. Visual aids, such as electronic magnifiers and smart glasses, enable individuals with low vision to access information and navigate their surroundings more effectively.

Telehealth and telemedicine have become integral components of the current state of assistive technologies, especially during times of crisis like the COVID-19 pandemic. Telehealth solutions enable remote medical consultations, monitoring, and intervention, ensuring continued care for aging individuals and those with mobility limitations.

Despite these significant advancements, challenges remain in the widespread adoption and accessibility of assistive technologies. Affordability, availability in rural areas, and digital literacy among older adults are some of the barriers that need to be addressed. Additionally, interoperability and data privacy concerns must be carefully managed to ensure the safe and ethical use of assistive technologies.

In "Tech and Aging: Enhancing Lives Through Assistive Technologies," we celebrate the current state of assistive technologies while acknowledging the work that lies ahead. By staying attuned to the needs of users, fostering collaboration among stakeholders, and leveraging emerging technologies, we can continue to push the boundaries of what assistive technologies can achieve. Together, we can create an inclusive and accessible world where technology empowers individuals of all ages and abilities to thrive and lead fulfilling lives.

CHAPTER IV
Types of Assistive Technologies for Aging Individuals

A. Mobility Assistance Devices

Mobility is a fundamental aspect of independent living, and as individuals age, maintaining mobility becomes increasingly crucial to their well-being and quality of life. Mobility assistance devices play a vital role in supporting aging individuals with mobility challenges, empowering them to move around safely and comfortably. In this section, we explore various types of mobility assistance devices that have revolutionized the lives of seniors.

❖ Walking Aids: Walking aids are among the most common and widely used mobility assistance devices for seniors. They provide support and stability while walking, helping older adults maintain balance and reduce the risk of falls. Some popular walking aids include:

a. Canes: Canes are lightweight and versatile, providing support to individuals who need assistance with balance but have relatively good mobility.

b. Walkers: Walkers come in various designs, including standard walkers with four legs, two-wheeled walkers, and rollators with four wheels and a seat. They offer more stability and support, making them suitable for individuals with moderate to severe mobility impairments.

❖ Wheelchairs: Wheelchairs are essential mobility devices for individuals with limited or no ability to walk. They come in different types, catering to various needs:

a. Manual Wheelchairs: Manual wheelchairs are propelled by the user or a caregiver through hand rims on the wheels. They are lightweight and easy to transport, making them suitable for both indoor and outdoor use.

b. Power Wheelchairs: Power wheelchairs are motorized and operated by a joystick or other control devices. They are ideal for individuals with limited upper body strength or dexterity.

c. Scooters: Mobility scooters are motorized devices

with handlebars and a seat, offering a more comfortable and efficient mode of transportation for outdoor use.

❖ Transfer Aids: Transfer aids are designed to assist seniors with transferring from one position to another, such as from a bed to a chair or a wheelchair. Some common transfer aids include:

a. Transfer Boards: Transfer boards are sturdy, flat boards that facilitate smooth transfers between surfaces.

b. Transfer Benches: Transfer benches have a seat that extends outside of the bathtub or shower, allowing seniors to sit down safely and slide into the bathing area.

❖ Stairlifts: Stairlifts are mechanical devices installed on staircases, allowing seniors to be seated while moving up or down the stairs. They are particularly beneficial for individuals with limited mobility in the lower body.

❖ Elevators and Lifts: Home elevators and lifts provide vertical transportation within multi-story homes, enabling older adults to access different levels without climbing stairs.

The current state of mobility assistance devices is marked by ongoing innovation and efforts to improve user experience. Lightweight materials, ergonomic designs, and advanced features have made these devices more convenient, user-friendly, and aesthetically pleasing. Additionally, assistive technologies, such as smart walkers with fall detection capabilities and GPS tracking, add an extra layer of safety for aging individuals and their caregivers.

In "Tech and Aging: Enhancing Lives Through Assistive Technologies," we delve into the transformative impact of mobility assistance devices, sharing real-life testimonials and success stories from seniors who have regained independence and confidence with the help of these technologies. By embracing and advocating for accessible mobility solutions, we can create a world where aging individuals can continue to explore and engage in the world around them, with the support and freedom they deserve.

B. Cognitive Support Technologies

Cognitive support technologies are a rapidly evolving category of assistive devices that cater to the unique needs of aging individuals with cognitive impairments. As people age, some may experience changes in memory, attention, and other cognitive functions. Cognitive support technologies aim to enhance cognitive abilities, promote mental stimulation, and enable older adults to maintain their independence and cognitive well-being. In this section, we explore various types of cognitive support technologies that have emerged to empower seniors in their daily lives.

❖ Memory Aids: Memory aids are designed to assist individuals with memory-related challenges, including forgetfulness and difficulty with organization. Some common memory aids include:

a. Reminders and Alarms: Digital devices, such as smartphones and smartwatches, can set reminders for appointments, medication schedules, and important tasks.

b. Digital Calendars: Digital calendars and task

management apps help seniors keep track of events, appointments, and daily routines.

c. Pill Organizers: Pill organizers with compartments for each day of the week or time of day ensure that seniors take the correct medications at the right time.

❖ Cognitive Games and Apps: A wide variety of cognitive games and apps are available to stimulate mental activity and memory retention. These apps offer puzzles, quizzes, memory games, and brain-training exercises that engage seniors' cognitive abilities and provide enjoyable mental stimulation.

❖ Communication Devices: For individuals with speech or language impairments, communication devices with text-to-speech and speech-to-text capabilities are valuable tools. These devices facilitate communication and enable seniors to express themselves more effectively.

❖ Cognitive Assistants and Smart Homes: Smart home technologies integrated with artificial intelligence serve as cognitive assistants for older adults. These systems can provide reminders, answer questions, and automate routine tasks, such as adjusting lighting or setting room temperatures.

❖ GPS Tracking and Wayfinding: GPS tracking and navigation apps are useful for older adults who may experience difficulty with wayfinding or have memory challenges related to locations. These apps can provide turn-by-turn directions and location-based reminders.

❖ Digital Memory Journals: Digital memory journals allow seniors to record their daily experiences, thoughts, and memories. These journals can help preserve personal histories and serve as therapeutic tools for individuals with cognitive impairments.

❖ Virtual Reality (VR) and Cognitive Rehabilitation: VR technology is being utilized in cognitive rehabilitation programs for individuals with cognitive decline or brain injuries. VR simulations provide cognitive exercises and activities that improve memory, attention, and problem-solving skills.

The rapid integration of artificial intelligence and machine learning in cognitive support technologies has significantly improved their efficacy. AI-powered systems can adapt to individual users' needs, monitor progress, and provide personalized support. Additionally, data analytics and pattern recognition allow these technologies to identify trends in cognitive functioning, helping caregivers and healthcare professionals make informed decisions regarding cognitive care.

In "Tech and Aging: Enhancing Lives Through Assistive Technologies," we explore the transformative potential of cognitive support technologies. Real-life case studies and testimonials demonstrate how these technologies have empowered older adults to live more fulfilling lives, fostering cognitive engagement, and promoting overall well-being. By embracing cognitive support technologies, we can enhance the cognitive health of aging individuals and support their continued participation and contribution to society.

C. Sensory Aids and Communication Tools

Sensory aids and communication tools are essential components of assistive technologies designed to support aging individuals with sensory impairments. As people age, their sensory functions, such as vision and hearing, may be affected, leading to challenges in communication and accessing information. Sensory aids and communication tools aim to bridge these gaps, enabling seniors to maintain social connections, access information, and engage more fully with the world around them. In this section, we explore various types of sensory aids and communication tools that have revolutionized the lives of older adults.

- ❖ Hearing Aids: Hearing aids are among the most common and effective sensory aids for individuals with hearing loss. These devices are designed to amplify sounds, making them more audible for the wearer. Modern hearing aids come in various styles, including behind-the-ear, in-the-ear, and completely-in-the-canal, offering discreet and comfortable options for users.

❖ Cochlear Implants: Cochlear implants are surgically implanted devices that provide direct electrical stimulation to the auditory nerve, bypassing damaged parts of the inner ear. These implants are suitable for individuals with severe to profound hearing loss and can significantly improve hearing and speech comprehension.

❖ Visual Aids: Visual aids cater to individuals with low vision or blindness, offering support in various daily activities. Some common visual aids include:

a. Magnifiers: Electronic magnifiers and handheld magnifying glasses help seniors read books, newspapers, and other printed materials with ease.

b. Screen Readers: Screen readers convert on-screen text into synthesized speech or Braille, enabling individuals with visual impairments to access digital content.

c. Braille Devices: Braille displays and Braille embossers provide access to written materials for individuals who read Braille.

❖ Tactile Communication Tools: Tactile communication tools facilitate communication for individuals with hearing and vision impairments. These tools include tactile sign language interpreters, tactile graphics, and tactile communication boards.

❖ Speech-to-Text and Text-to-Speech Applications: Speech-to-text and text-to-speech applications are valuable communication tools for individuals with speech or hearing impairments. These applications convert spoken words into text or vice versa, enhancing communication with others.

❖ Video Relay Services: Video relay services enable individuals with hearing impairments to communicate over the telephone using sign language interpreters. The interpreter relays the conversation between the deaf user and the hearing party.

❖ Communication Apps: Communication apps, including video conferencing tools and messaging platforms, have become indispensable for seniors to stay connected with family and friends, especially during times of social distancing.

❖ Haptic Feedback Devices: Haptic feedback devices provide tactile sensations, enhancing the sensory experience for individuals with visual or hearing impairments. They can convey information through vibrations or touch-based cues.

The current state of sensory aids and communication tools is characterized by user-friendly designs and seamless integration with digital technologies. These assistive devices and applications empower older adults with sensory impairments to maintain independence, participate actively in social interactions, and access information in ways that were previously challenging.

In "Tech and Aging: Enhancing Lives Through Assistive Technologies," we celebrate the transformative impact of sensory aids and communication tools. Through real-life success stories and testimonials, we witness how these technologies have enriched the lives of seniors, fostering communication, social connectivity, and greater independence. By embracing and promoting the accessibility of sensory aids and communication tools, we can create a more inclusive and supportive environment for aging individuals, ensuring that they remain active and engaged members of their communities.

D. Health Monitoring and Telehealth Solutions

Health monitoring and telehealth solutions are revolutionizing the way healthcare is delivered to aging individuals. These assistive technologies offer real-time monitoring, remote medical consultations, and proactive health management, empowering seniors to take charge of their well-being and receive timely healthcare support. In this section, we explore various types of health monitoring and telehealth solutions that have transformed the landscape of healthcare for older adults.

- ❖ Wearable Health Monitors: Wearable health monitors, such as fitness trackers and smartwatches, are popular devices among seniors for tracking vital signs, physical activity, and sleep patterns. These devices provide valuable insights into health metrics, enabling seniors to monitor their well-being and share data with healthcare providers for remote assessment.

❖ Remote Patient Monitoring (RPM) Devices: RPM devices are designed to continuously monitor specific health parameters and transmit data to healthcare professionals for review. RPM devices can monitor conditions such as blood pressure, glucose levels, and heart rate, allowing healthcare providers to detect trends and intervene promptly when necessary.

❖ Medication Management Tools: Medication management tools help seniors adhere to their medication schedules and reduce the risk of medication errors. These tools include smart pill organizers with alarms, medication reminder apps, and devices that dispense medications at scheduled times.

❖ Telehealth Platforms: Telehealth platforms facilitate virtual medical consultations between seniors and healthcare providers. Video conferencing and remote communication technologies allow seniors to discuss health concerns, receive medical advice, and even obtain prescriptions without leaving their homes.

❖ Remote Diagnostics and Testing: Remote diagnostic devices enable seniors to conduct certain medical tests at home, with the results transmitted to healthcare providers for analysis. These devices may include remote blood glucose monitors, home blood pressure cuffs, and at-home urine analysis kits.

❖ Emergency Response Systems: Emergency response systems, often known as personal emergency response systems (PERS), provide seniors with a quick and easy way to call for help in emergencies. These systems typically consist of wearable buttons or devices that connect to a monitoring center, where trained operators can dispatch assistance when needed.

❖ Telemedicine Robots: Telemedicine robots equipped with video conferencing capabilities allow healthcare providers to interact with seniors in remote or assisted living facilities. These robots enable more personalized and responsive care delivery, reducing the need for in-person visits.

❖ Remote Rehabilitation Programs: Telehealth extends to rehabilitation services, providing seniors with remote access to physical therapy, occupational therapy, and speech therapy sessions. These programs help seniors recover from injuries, surgeries, or strokes from the comfort of their homes.

The integration of health monitoring and telehealth solutions into the lives of seniors has proven particularly valuable, especially during times of global health crises. Telehealth has become a vital tool for ensuring continued access to medical care while minimizing exposure to infectious diseases.

In "Tech and Aging: Enhancing Lives Through Assistive Technologies," we celebrate the transformative power of health monitoring and telehealth solutions. Through real-life success stories, we witness how these technologies have improved healthcare outcomes, enhanced preventive care, and empowered seniors to actively manage their health. By embracing and expanding the use of health monitoring and telehealth solutions, we can create a future where seniors can age in place, access high-quality healthcare, and enjoy a greater sense of well-being and autonomy in their later years.

CHAPTER V
Integrating Tech and Aging: Overcoming Barriers

A. Accessibility and Inclusivity Challenges

As technology continues to advance, the integration of tech and aging holds immense promise for enhancing the lives of older adults. However, several barriers related to accessibility and inclusivity must be addressed to ensure that these technologies benefit all seniors, regardless of their abilities or technological literacy.

- ❖ Digital Divide: The digital divide refers to the gap in access to and use of technology between different demographic groups. Many older adults, particularly those in underserved communities, may lack access to high-speed internet and digital devices. Bridging the digital divide requires efforts to make technology more affordable and accessible to seniors, especially those with limited financial resources.

- ❖ Technological Literacy: Some older adults may experience challenges in adopting and using new technologies due to limited technological literacy. User interfaces and interactions must be designed with older adults in mind, taking into account factors like font size, color contrast, and intuitive navigation. User-friendly technology can empower seniors to embrace and benefit from assistive technologies.

❖ Ageism and Stigma: Ageism and stigma surrounding aging and disability can influence the acceptance and adoption of assistive technologies. Creating awareness and promoting positive attitudes toward aging and disability are crucial steps in fostering an inclusive environment where seniors feel comfortable using these technologies.

❖ Complex Interfaces: Many technologies, including smartphones and computers, can have complex interfaces that may be overwhelming for some seniors. Simplifying interfaces and providing step-by-step guidance can make technology more approachable and less intimidating.

❖ Physical Accessibility: Physical accessibility is essential in ensuring that assistive technologies are usable by individuals with mobility challenges. Devices and interfaces should be designed with ergonomic considerations, accommodating users with different physical abilities.

❖ Lack of Standardization: The lack of standardization in assistive technologies can lead to compatibility issues and confusion for users. Implementing industry standards for accessibility and compatibility can streamline the adoption and use of these technologies.

❖ Privacy and Data Security Concerns: Many seniors express concerns about data privacy and security when using technology. Ensuring robust data protection measures and transparent privacy policies is crucial in building trust and encouraging adoption.

❖ Lack of Awareness: Some older adults may not be aware of the full range of assistive technologies available to them. Raising awareness through educational programs, workshops, and community outreach can help older adults and caregivers understand the potential benefits of these technologies.

❖ Connectivity and Reliability: For technologies that rely on internet connectivity or remote services, issues like network reliability and connectivity challenges can hinder their effectiveness. Ensuring stable and reliable connections is essential, especially for telehealth and remote monitoring solutions.

Overcoming these accessibility and inclusivity challenges requires a multi-faceted approach involving collaboration among technology developers, healthcare providers, policymakers, and advocacy organizations. Human-centered design principles, user testing, and feedback from older adults are essential in creating technologies that truly cater to their needs and preferences.

In "Tech and Aging: Enhancing Lives Through Assistive Technologies," we explore the efforts and initiatives aimed at overcoming these barriers. By addressing these challenges head-on, we can pave the way for a future where technology seamlessly integrates with aging, enabling seniors to lead more independent, healthy, and fulfilling lives in the digital age.

B. User Experience and User-Centered Design

User experience (UX) and user-centered design (UCD) play a pivotal role in successfully integrating technology and aging. These principles ensure that assistive technologies are designed with the end-user, specifically older adults, in mind. By prioritizing UX and UCD, developers can create intuitive, accessible, and inclusive technologies that cater to the unique needs and preferences of seniors.

❖ Understanding User Needs: A fundamental aspect of UCD is gaining a deep understanding of the needs, abilities, and challenges faced by older adults. User research, including surveys, interviews, and focus groups, allows developers to gather valuable insights that inform the design process. Understanding user needs is the foundation for creating technologies that address real-world problems faced by seniors.

❖ Simplicity and Intuitiveness: Many older adults may be less familiar with technology, so simplicity and intuitiveness are paramount. Designers should avoid complex jargon, reduce cognitive load, and create clear and concise user interfaces. By minimizing unnecessary steps and offering straightforward interactions, seniors can more easily navigate and use assistive technologies.

❖ Font Size and Color Contrast: Visual impairments are common among older adults, making font size and color contrast critical design considerations. Using legible fonts and ensuring sufficient contrast between text and background enhances readability for seniors with low vision.

❖ Inclusive Interfaces: Inclusivity involves accommodating a diverse user base with varying abilities and needs. Assistive technologies should offer multiple input options, such as touch, voice commands, and gestures, to cater to users with different physical capabilities.

❖ Flexibility and Customization: Personalization is key to user satisfaction. Offering customization options allows seniors to adapt the technology to their preferences and requirements. Adjustable font sizes, color themes, and voice settings can significantly improve the user experience.

❖ Empowering Autonomy: User-centered design should prioritize empowering seniors to retain control and autonomy over their technology use. Avoiding excessive automation and providing options for manual control can give seniors a sense of agency and independence.

❖ Iterative Design Process: The iterative design process involves continually gathering feedback from users and making incremental improvements to the technology based on that feedback. This approach ensures that the technology evolves to meet the changing needs and expectations of seniors.

- ❖ Usability Testing: Usability testing involves observing how seniors interact with the technology and identifying pain points or usability issues. Testing with older adults in real-world scenarios helps identify design flaws and areas for improvement.

- ❖ Collaboration with Older Adults: Including older adults in the design and development process is essential. Co-designing with seniors ensures that their voices are heard, and their perspectives shape the technology they will be using. Participatory design workshops can foster collaboration and creative problem-solving.

By embracing UX and UCD principles, developers can create assistive technologies that seniors find approachable, engaging, and beneficial. Moreover, adopting these principles ensures that the resulting technologies align with the goals of enhancing seniors' lives, promoting independence, and fostering social connectivity.

In "Tech and Aging: Enhancing Lives Through Assistive Technologies," we delve into the importance of UX and

UCD in overcoming barriers. Through real-life case studies and success stories, we witness how user-centered design has made a profound impact on the lives of older adults. By continuously refining and enhancing the user experience, we can create a future where technology seamlessly integrates with aging, enriching the lives of seniors and promoting a more inclusive and accessible society.

C. Addressing Privacy and Ethical Concerns

As technology becomes increasingly intertwined with the lives of older adults, addressing privacy and ethical concerns is paramount in ensuring the responsible integration of tech and aging. Assistive technologies may collect sensitive personal data and interact closely with users, making it essential to safeguard privacy and uphold ethical principles. In this section, we explore key considerations for mitigating privacy risks and navigating ethical challenges.

❖ Data Security and Confidentiality: Protecting the privacy of seniors' data should be a top priority. Technology developers must implement robust data security measures, including encryption, access controls, and secure storage practices. Furthermore, transparent privacy policies and informed consent procedures should be in place to clarify how data will be used and shared.

❖ User Consent and Control: Obtaining informed consent from older adults is crucial before collecting their personal data. Seniors should have control over the information they share and the ability to revoke consent at any time. User-friendly interfaces can allow seniors to easily manage their data preferences and exercise control over their information.

❖ Anonymization and De-identification: Where possible, anonymizing or de-identifying data can help protect user privacy. By removing or encrypting personally identifiable information, developers can still analyze aggregated data trends without compromising individual privacy.

❖ Transparent Data Practices: Transparency in data practices builds trust between users and technology providers. Clearly communicating how data will be used, who will have access to it, and the purposes of data collection can help seniors make informed decisions about using the technology.

❖ Cybersecurity: The risk of cyber threats and data breaches is a significant concern in the digital age. Technology developers should prioritize cybersecurity measures, including regular software updates, vulnerability assessments, and employee training on best security practices.

❖ Ethical AI and Decision-Making: When artificial intelligence (AI) is integrated into assistive technologies, ethical considerations come into play. Ensuring that AI algorithms are unbiased, fair, and do not reinforce discriminatory practices is essential in providing equitable support to all users.

❖ Preventing Ageism and Discrimination: Technology developers must be vigilant in avoiding ageism and discrimination in the design and functionality of assistive technologies. Creating inclusive and unbiased technologies that cater to the diverse needs of older adults is essential for promoting equitable access.

❖ End-of-Life and Legacy Data: Addressing what happens to user data after the individual's passing is an ethical consideration often overlooked. Developers should provide options for end-of-life data management or allow users to designate data custodians who can handle their data responsibly.

❖ Human Oversight and Accountability: While technology can enhance aging experiences, human oversight is necessary to ensure ethical decision-making and intervention when needed. Technology providers should establish mechanisms for accountability and intervention in case of system errors or inappropriate use.

By taking a proactive approach to privacy and ethical concerns, technology developers can foster a culture of responsible innovation and demonstrate a commitment to users' well-being. Responsible tech integration promotes user trust, encourages broader adoption of assistive technologies, and ultimately improves the quality of life for older adults.

In "Tech and Aging: Enhancing Lives Through Assistive Technologies," we delve into the significance of addressing privacy and ethical concerns in the tech and aging landscape. Through real-life case studies and expert insights, we explore how ethical practices enhance user experiences and foster a sense of confidence and security among seniors. By upholding privacy and ethical principles, we can create a future where technology supports aging individuals in ways that are respectful, empowering, and aligned with their values and preferences.

CHAPTER VI
Case Studies: Real-Life Impact of Assistive Technologies

A. Personal Testimonials and Success Stories

The real-life impact of assistive technologies on the lives of older adults is best captured through personal testimonials and success stories. These heartwarming accounts illustrate how technology has empowered seniors to overcome challenges, enhance their independence, and lead fulfilling lives. In this section, we present a selection of personal testimonials that showcase the transformative power of assistive technologies.

❖ Testimonial from Sarah Thompson (72): "Before I discovered my smartwatch with a fall detection feature, I was constantly worried about falling and not being able to call for help. My children were concerned about my safety, especially when I was alone. But ever since I started wearing this watch, I feel more confident going about my daily activities. It gives me peace of mind knowing that if I ever need assistance, all I have to do is press a button, and help will be on the way. It's like having a guardian angel right on my wrist!"

❖ Testimonial from James and Mary Johnson (80 and 78, respectively): "Our hearing loss made conversations with our family and friends a real struggle. We felt isolated and disconnected. However, after getting hearing aids with Bluetooth connectivity, everything changed! Now we can hear our loved ones clearly during phone calls and video chats. It's like a whole new world has opened up to us. We no longer feel left out during family gatherings or social events. These hearing aids have truly reconnected us with our loved ones and brought joy back into our lives."

❖ Testimonial from Robert Ramirez (85): "After my stroke, I thought I might never walk again. But with my robotic exoskeleton, I am making incredible progress in my rehabilitation journey. This amazing device has given me the strength and support to stand and walk again. The feeling of taking steps on my own is indescribable. It's like a second chance at life. I'm grateful to the technology and the dedicated therapists who have helped me regain my mobility and independence."

❖ Testimonial from Susan Anderson (68): "I used to struggle with remembering to take my medications properly. But ever since I started using a medication management app on my smartphone, it's been a game-changer. I get timely reminders for each dose, and the app even tracks my medication adherence. It has helped me stay on top of my health and avoid any missed doses. I feel more in control of managing my health, and my doctor has noticed a positive change in my overall well-being."

❖ Testimonial from Henry Lee (92): "Being visually impaired, I thought reading was a thing of the past. But then my granddaughter introduced me to a handheld electronic magnifier. It's like having a magic magnifying glass! I can now read my favorite books, letters from friends, and even my recipes in the kitchen. This device has reignited my love for reading, and I feel more independent, even at my age. I can't thank technology enough for this wonderful gift."

These personal testimonials offer a glimpse into the profound impact that assistive technologies have on the lives of older adults. From enhancing safety and communication to promoting mobility and social engagement, these technologies have become indispensable companions for seniors on their aging journey. As technology continues to evolve, we can expect even more inspiring stories of how innovation empowers older adults to age with dignity, independence, and joy.

In "Tech and Aging: Enhancing Lives Through Assistive Technologies," we celebrate the real-life impact of assistive technologies by sharing more personal testimonials and success stories. These heartwarming accounts inspire us to continue embracing technology as a powerful tool for enhancing the lives of seniors and promoting a more inclusive and age-friendly society.

B. Case Studies from Various Age Groups and Conditions

The impact of assistive technologies extends beyond older adults, benefiting individuals of different age groups and conditions. These inspiring case studies highlight how technology has transformed the lives of people with diverse abilities, opening new possibilities and opportunities for independence. In this section, we present a selection of case studies that showcase the real-life impact of assistive technologies on individuals with various age groups and conditions.

❖ Case Study: Emma Martinez (10): Emma was born with cerebral palsy, which severely limited her mobility. She could not walk without assistance and struggled with everyday tasks. However, after receiving a motorized wheelchair with customizable controls, Emma's world transformed. Now, she can independently move around her school and participate in sports activities with her friends. The wheelchair's lightweight design and responsive controls have given Emma newfound freedom and confidence.

- ❖ Case Study: David Johnson (30): David suffered a traumatic brain injury in a car accident, which affected his memory and speech. With the help of a communication device equipped with a text-to-speech function, David can now express his thoughts and feelings effectively. The device's intuitive interface and pre-programmed phrases allow David to communicate with his family, friends, and medical professionals, enriching his social interactions and improving his overall well-being.

- ❖ Case Study: Maya Patel (45): Maya was diagnosed with early-onset Alzheimer's disease, which gradually impacted her memory and cognitive abilities. Her family introduced her to a smart home system with voice-controlled features. Now, Maya can control her home environment, such as adjusting the thermostat, turning on lights, and locking doors, all through voice commands. The smart home system has reduced her reliance on others and improved her sense of independence and dignity.

❖ Case Study: Michael Turner (55): Michael has low vision due to retinitis pigmentosa. He struggled to read printed materials and navigate unfamiliar places. With the help of electronic magnifiers and a navigation app with audio instructions, Michael can now read restaurant menus, bus schedules, and street signs more easily. The technology has enabled him to explore new places confidently and participate more actively in his community.

❖ Case Study: Laura Mitchell (70): Laura lives in a remote area with limited access to healthcare facilities. However, with the introduction of telehealth services, Laura can now consult with her doctor through video calls. Her chronic condition is managed efficiently, and she receives timely medical advice from the comfort of her home. Telehealth has revolutionized Laura's access to healthcare, providing convenience and continuity of care.

❖ Case Study: Jack and Emily Baker (80 and 78, respectively): Jack and Emily, a couple married for over 50 years, faced hearing loss as they aged. To maintain their connection, they decided to get hearing aids with Bluetooth capabilities. Now, they can stream music and audio from their favorite shows directly to their hearing aids. The hearing aids have enhanced their shared experiences and rekindled their joy in music and storytelling.

These case studies illustrate the transformative power of assistive technologies across different age groups and conditions. From young children with mobility impairments to older adults with sensory challenges, technology has become a vital enabler of independence, communication, and social engagement. As technology continues to advance, we can expect even more innovative solutions that enhance the lives of individuals with diverse abilities, enriching their experiences and fostering inclusion in society.

In "Tech and Aging: Enhancing Lives Through Assistive Technologies," we celebrate these diverse case studies, highlighting the versatility and impact of assistive technologies across generations. These real-life stories motivate us to continue advocating for accessible and inclusive technology solutions, ensuring that everyone, regardless of age or condition, can benefit from the life-changing potential of assistive technologies.

CHAPTER VII
Emerging Trends in Assistive Technologies

A. AI and Machine Learning Applications

The emergence of artificial intelligence (AI) and machine learning (ML) has paved the way for groundbreaking advancements in assistive technologies. These technologies have the potential to revolutionize the support and care provided to aging individuals and people with disabilities. By harnessing the power of AI and ML, assistive technologies are becoming more intelligent, personalized, and effective in addressing individual needs and challenges.

❖ Personalized Support: AI and ML algorithms can analyze vast amounts of data to understand users' preferences, habits, and unique requirements. This allows assistive technologies to offer personalized support tailored to each individual's specific needs. Whether it's adaptive interfaces, customized health monitoring, or personalized reminders, AI-driven systems can adapt to the user's changing circumstances and provide more effective assistance.

❖ Natural Language Processing (NLP): NLP enables assistive technologies to understand and process human language, making communication more intuitive and seamless. Voice-activated assistants equipped with NLP capabilities can respond to spoken commands, answer questions, and perform tasks, enabling seniors to interact with technology effortlessly.

❖ Predictive Analytics: AI-powered assistive technologies can use predictive analytics to anticipate users' needs and behaviors. For example, predictive algorithms can anticipate falls based on gait patterns and alert caregivers or emergency services in advance. By being proactive, these technologies can prevent accidents and improve overall safety.

❖ Advanced Robotics: AI-driven robotics is revolutionizing mobility assistance for seniors and individuals with mobility impairments. Robotic exoskeletons and smart walking aids use ML algorithms to adapt their movements to the user's gait, providing personalized support and enhancing mobility.

❖ Cognitive Support: AI and ML play a crucial role in cognitive support technologies for aging individuals. These technologies can track cognitive health, detect early signs of cognitive decline, and offer cognitive training exercises tailored to the user's abilities. Cognitive support tools can promote brain health and delay the onset of cognitive impairments.

❖ Remote Monitoring and Diagnostics: AI-enabled remote monitoring systems can continuously analyze health data from wearables and other monitoring devices. ML algorithms can detect anomalies and patterns indicative of health issues, allowing for early intervention and remote diagnostics. This is especially valuable for seniors living in remote areas or those with limited access to healthcare facilities.

❖ Smart Home Integration: AI-powered smart home systems can learn users' routines and preferences, automating various tasks and adapting the home environment to their needs. Smart home integration enhances safety and comfort, allowing seniors to age in place more comfortably and independently.

❖ Social Interaction and Companionship: AI-driven social robots are designed to provide companionship and emotional support to seniors. These robots can engage in conversations, play games, and assist with tasks, reducing feelings of loneliness and isolation.

❖ Real-Time Translation and Accessibility: AI-driven translation services facilitate communication between seniors who speak different languages, making social interactions and travel more accessible and enjoyable. AI can also help make digital content more accessible through real-time captioning and audio descriptions for those with sensory impairments.

As AI and ML technologies continue to evolve, so will the capabilities of assistive technologies. The integration of AI in assistive devices holds immense promise in transforming the lives of aging individuals and individuals with disabilities, enabling them to lead more independent, empowered, and connected lives.

In "Tech and Aging: Enhancing Lives Through Assistive Technologies," we explore the potential of AI and ML in transforming assistive technologies. By embracing these emerging trends, we can drive innovation, foster inclusivity, and create a future where technology serves as a powerful ally in enhancing the quality of life for people of all abilities.

B. Robotics and Companion Devices

The advent of robotics and companion devices is ushering in a new era of assistive technologies that provide not only practical support but also emotional companionship. Robotics, combined with AI and advanced sensors, offers a range of devices that cater to the unique needs of aging individuals and people with disabilities. From robotic assistants to social companions, these technologies are transforming the landscape of care and support for vulnerable populations.

- ❖ Robotic Assistants: Robotic assistants are designed to perform a variety of tasks to assist aging individuals and individuals with mobility challenges. These robots can help with household chores such as cleaning, cooking, and carrying items. They can also assist with personal care, such as helping with dressing and grooming. Robotic assistants provide a level of independence and support that can significantly improve the quality of life for seniors and individuals with disabilities.

- ❖ Smart Walking Aids: Smart walking aids combine robotics and advanced sensors to provide personalized support for individuals with mobility impairments. These devices can adapt their movements to the user's gait, providing stability and assistance during walking. They are particularly beneficial for seniors with balance issues or those recovering from injuries.

❖ Robotic Exoskeletons: Robotic exoskeletons are wearable devices that augment a person's physical capabilities. They can assist with standing, walking, and performing various movements. These exoskeletons are especially valuable for individuals with spinal cord injuries or neuromuscular conditions, enabling them to regain mobility and participate more actively in daily activities.

❖ Social Robots: Social robots are designed to provide emotional companionship and engage in social interactions with users. These robots can recognize and respond to human emotions, engage in conversations, and even provide entertainment through games and activities. Social robots offer a sense of companionship, reduce feelings of loneliness, and promote emotional well-being, especially for seniors living alone or in care facilities.

❖ Robotic Pets: Robotic pets offer the joy and comfort of companionship without the responsibilities of caring for a live animal. These lifelike robotic pets can respond to touch and interaction, providing comfort and emotional support. Robotic pets have been shown to reduce stress and anxiety and can be particularly beneficial for individuals with dementia or Alzheimer's.

❖ Telepresence Robots: Telepresence robots allow remote interaction and communication with family members, friends, and caregivers. These robots have a screen or display that enables real-time video conferencing and two-way communication. Telepresence robots enable distant family members to virtually visit their loved ones, providing a meaningful and interactive way to stay connected.

❖ Robotic Therapy Assistants: Robotic therapy assistants are used in physical and occupational therapy to support rehabilitation and exercise programs. These robots can guide users through therapeutic exercises, provide feedback on performance, and track progress over time. Robotic therapy assistants enhance the effectiveness of therapy and encourage active participation in the recovery process.

❖ **AI-Enhanced Companions:** AI-powered companions leverage natural language processing and emotional intelligence to engage in conversations and provide emotional support. These companions can respond to users' feelings, offer encouragement, and serve as a source of comfort during difficult times. AI-enhanced companions are valuable for individuals who may not have regular social interactions or those in need of emotional support.

As robotics and companion devices continue to advance, they hold the potential to address the growing need for personalized and compassionate care for aging populations and individuals with disabilities. These technologies not only provide practical assistance but also foster emotional well-being, independence, and a sense of connection with others.

In "Tech and Aging: Enhancing Lives Through Assistive Technologies," we explore the transformative role of robotics and companion devices. By embracing these emerging trends, we can pave the way for a future where technology nurtures a compassionate and inclusive environment, enriching the lives of vulnerable populations and empowering them to thrive with dignity and joy.

C. Virtual Reality and Augmented Reality Solutions

Virtual Reality (VR) and Augmented Reality (AR) are rapidly emerging as transformative technologies in the field of assistive solutions. These immersive technologies offer new ways to enhance the lives of aging individuals and people with disabilities, providing innovative solutions for training, therapy, and accessibility. By blurring the line between the physical and digital worlds, VR and AR open up exciting possibilities for inclusive and empowering experiences.

❖ VR for Therapy and Rehabilitation: Virtual Reality is revolutionizing the way therapy and rehabilitation are delivered. In physical therapy, VR can simulate real-world scenarios to help individuals regain motor skills and balance. For cognitive therapy, VR can be used to create stimulating environments to enhance memory, attention, and problem-solving skills. The immersive nature of VR provides a safe and controlled space for therapeutic interventions.

❖ AR for Visual Assistance: AR solutions offer real-time information and visual assistance to users, making the world more accessible for individuals with visual impairments. AR glasses or smartphone apps can identify objects, recognize text, and provide audio cues to help users navigate their surroundings more independently. AR empowers individuals with visual challenges to recognize faces, read labels, and perform daily tasks with greater confidence.

❖ VR and AR for Social Interaction: VR and AR technologies have the potential to bridge the social gap for individuals with mobility limitations or those living in remote areas. Virtual reality environments can facilitate social gatherings, meetings, and events, enabling people to connect and interact from the comfort of their homes. AR can enhance face-to-face interactions by providing real-time translation or offering additional information about the person being spoken to.

❖ VR for Pain Management: VR has proven effective in pain management, providing a distraction from discomfort and promoting relaxation. Virtual reality experiences, such as serene landscapes or interactive games, can help individuals cope with chronic pain or discomfort during medical procedures. VR therapy reduces the reliance on medication and offers a drug-free alternative for pain relief.

❖ AR for Learning Support: Augmented Reality can enhance the learning experience for individuals with learning disabilities or cognitive challenges. AR applications can provide interactive visual aids, illustrate complex concepts, and offer step-by-step guidance for learning new skills. AR-based learning tools cater to diverse learning styles and make education more engaging and accessible.

❖ VR for Empathy and Training: Virtual Reality is being utilized to promote empathy and understanding for individuals with different abilities. VR simulations can put users in the shoes of others, helping them experience life from the perspective of someone with disabilities. This immersive experience fosters empathy, reduces stigma, and promotes a more inclusive society.

❖ AR for Navigation and Wayfinding: AR-based navigation applications assist individuals with spatial orientation and wayfinding challenges. AR overlays on maps or indoor environments provide turn-by-turn directions and visual cues to guide users to their destinations. AR wayfinding empowers individuals to explore new places with confidence and independence.

❖ VR for Mindfulness and Mental Health: Virtual Reality offers mindfulness experiences that promote relaxation, stress reduction, and emotional well-being. VR environments can transport users to tranquil settings for meditation or provide interactive experiences for managing anxiety and stress. VR mindfulness sessions offer a calming escape from the pressures of daily life.

As VR and AR technologies continue to advance, their potential to empower and enrich the lives of aging individuals and people with disabilities will only grow. These immersive technologies hold the promise of transforming the way we approach therapy, accessibility, education, and social interaction, fostering a more inclusive and supportive world for all.

In "Tech and Aging: Enhancing Lives Through Assistive Technologies," we explore the transformative role of Virtual Reality and Augmented Reality solutions. By embracing these emerging trends, we can harness the power of immersive experiences to promote well-being, foster empathy, and create an environment where technology becomes an empowering ally for individuals of all abilities.

CHAPTER VIII
The Role of Caregivers and Healthcare Professionals

A. Empowering Caregivers through Technology

Caregivers play a crucial role in supporting aging individuals and those with disabilities. The demands of caregiving can be physically and emotionally challenging, and technology has emerged as a powerful ally in easing these burdens and enhancing the caregiving experience. From digital tools that streamline caregiving tasks to remote monitoring solutions, technology empowers caregivers with valuable resources and support.

- ❖ Care Coordination Platforms: Technology offers care coordination platforms that enable caregivers to organize and manage the care of their loved ones efficiently. These platforms provide a centralized hub for sharing medical records, appointments, and medication schedules. Caregivers can collaborate with healthcare professionals and family members, ensuring that everyone is on the same page regarding the individual's care.

❖ Mobile Apps for Medication Management: Medication management apps offer caregivers a simple and effective way to track and administer medications. These apps provide reminders for dosage times, drug interactions, and refills. Caregivers can easily monitor medication adherence and ensure their loved ones receive their prescribed treatments on time.

❖ Remote Monitoring Devices: Remote monitoring devices allow caregivers to keep track of their loved one's health from a distance. These devices can measure vital signs, activity levels, and sleep patterns, providing valuable insights into the individual's overall well-being. Remote monitoring offers peace of mind to caregivers, enabling them to respond promptly to any changes in their loved one's health.

❖ Video Conferencing for Telehealth: Video conferencing technology enables caregivers to participate in virtual doctor appointments or telehealth consultations. This remote access to healthcare professionals saves time and reduces the need for travel, especially for seniors who may have mobility challenges. Caregivers can actively engage in discussions about their loved one's health and treatment plans.

❖ GPS Tracking and Safety Devices: GPS tracking devices and safety wearables offer an added layer of security for caregivers. These devices allow caregivers to locate their loved ones in case of wandering or emergency situations. Safety wearables with built-in fall detection can alert caregivers or emergency services if a fall occurs.

❖ Communication and Social Apps: Technology facilitates communication and social connection for caregivers and their loved ones. Messaging apps, video calls, and social media platforms enable regular interactions and reduce feelings of isolation, especially for long-distance caregivers. Staying connected fosters emotional well-being for both the caregiver and the individual receiving care.

❖ Virtual Support Groups: Virtual support groups provide caregivers with opportunities to connect with others facing similar challenges. Online forums and virtual meetings offer a safe space for sharing experiences, exchanging advice, and seeking emotional support. Caregivers benefit from the sense of community and understanding that these virtual groups provide.

❖ AI-Powered Decision Support: AI-driven decision support systems offer caregivers evidence-based information and resources for making informed decisions about care. These systems can provide suggestions for managing specific health conditions, handling common caregiving challenges, and accessing relevant educational materials.

By embracing technology, caregivers gain access to tools and resources that enhance their caregiving capabilities and overall well-being. Technology not only streamlines caregiving tasks but also reduces stress and isolation, empowering caregivers to provide the best possible care for their loved ones. As technology continues to evolve, caregivers will have even more innovative solutions to support their caregiving journey and maintain their own health and resilience.

In "Tech and Aging: Enhancing Lives Through Assistive Technologies," we explore the pivotal role of technology in empowering caregivers. Through real-life stories and expert insights, we showcase how technology strengthens the caregiving bond, improves care coordination, and fosters a more supportive caregiving environment. By supporting caregivers with technology, we can uplift the quality of care provided to aging individuals and individuals with disabilities, ensuring that they receive the compassionate support they deserve.

B. Training and Support for Healthcare Providers

In the rapidly evolving landscape of assistive technologies, it is essential to equip healthcare professionals with the necessary training and support to effectively integrate these technologies into their practice. As technology becomes more prevalent in healthcare settings, healthcare providers play a pivotal role in identifying and implementing the most suitable assistive solutions for their patients. To ensure optimal care and outcomes, ongoing training, and support for healthcare professionals are crucial.

❖ Training on Assistive Technologies: Healthcare providers need comprehensive training on the latest assistive technologies available to support aging individuals and people with disabilities. Workshops, webinars, and hands-on training sessions can familiarize providers with various devices and applications, allowing them to make informed recommendations to their patients. This training ensures that healthcare professionals are up-to-date with the rapidly advancing landscape of assistive solutions.

❖ Understanding Patient Needs: Assistive technologies are most effective when tailored to the unique needs and preferences of individual patients. Healthcare providers should receive training on conducting thorough assessments of their patients' abilities and challenges. By understanding the specific requirements of their patients, providers can better match them with the appropriate assistive technologies that enhance their quality of life.

❖ Interdisciplinary Collaboration: Assistive technologies often require collaboration among various healthcare disciplines, including occupational therapists, physical therapists, speech-language pathologists, and technologists. Training should emphasize the importance of interdisciplinary teamwork, encouraging healthcare professionals to work together to develop comprehensive care plans that incorporate assistive technologies.

❖ Data Privacy and Ethics: As healthcare professionals integrate assistive technologies that collect and analyze patient data, training on data privacy and ethics is essential. Healthcare providers must understand the legal and ethical implications of handling patient information and ensure compliance with relevant privacy regulations. Patient consent, data security, and responsible data use should be integral components of their training.

❖ Keeping Up with Innovations: The field of assistive technologies is continually evolving, with new devices and applications being introduced regularly. Continuous education and professional development programs should be available to healthcare providers to keep them informed about the latest innovations and advancements. Staying updated allows providers to offer the most cutting-edge and effective solutions to their patients.

❖ Evidenced-Based Practice: Training should emphasize the importance of evidence-based practice in selecting and recommending assistive technologies. Healthcare professionals should have access to research and clinical studies that demonstrate the efficacy and benefits of specific technologies. This evidence-based approach instills confidence in providers as they make informed decisions about incorporating assistive technologies into patient care.

❖ Troubleshooting and Technical Support: Healthcare providers should receive training on troubleshooting common issues with assistive technologies and providing basic technical support to their patients. Familiarity with technical aspects ensures that healthcare professionals can address minor problems promptly, reducing potential barriers to technology adoption for patients.

❖ Addressing Patient Concerns: As with any new intervention, patients may have concerns or reservations about using assistive technologies. Training should prepare healthcare providers to address these concerns effectively. Providers can offer guidance, answer questions, and highlight the potential benefits of using assistive technologies to alleviate patient apprehension.

By investing in comprehensive training and ongoing support for healthcare professionals, the integration of assistive technologies into clinical practice can be seamless and successful. Empowered with the knowledge and skills to navigate the world of assistive solutions, healthcare providers become advocates for their patients' well-being and champions of inclusive and personalized care.

In "Tech and Aging: Enhancing Lives Through Assistive Technologies," we emphasize the critical role of healthcare professionals in the successful adoption of assistive technologies. Through real-life case studies and expert insights, we showcase how training and support empower healthcare providers to leverage technology to its fullest potential, ultimately benefiting the lives of their patients and enhancing the quality of care provided.

C. Collaborative Care Models with Technology

Collaboration between caregivers and healthcare professionals is essential for providing comprehensive and patient-centered care. Technology plays a pivotal role in facilitating seamless communication and information sharing among the care team. Collaborative care models leverage technology to create a unified approach to patient care, leading to improved outcomes, enhanced patient satisfaction, and better overall healthcare experiences.

❖ Electronic Health Records (EHRs): Electronic Health Records are at the core of collaborative care models. EHRs allow healthcare providers and caregivers to access and update patient information in real-time. This shared platform ensures that all members of the care team have access to the latest medical data, enabling coordinated decision-making and continuity of care.

❖ Telemedicine and Virtual Consultations: Telemedicine and virtual consultations have become integral to collaborative care models, especially in remote or underserved areas. Through video conferencing, healthcare professionals can conduct virtual appointments with patients and consult with other specialists and caregivers, regardless of geographical distances. Telemedicine enhances communication, facilitates timely interventions, and reduces the need for physical visits.

❖ Care Team Communication Apps: Specialized care team communication apps streamline communication among caregivers, healthcare professionals, and other members of the care team. These apps allow secure messaging, file sharing, and task assignment, ensuring that everyone involved in the patient's care stays informed and connected.

❖ Real-Time Alerts and Notifications: Technology enables real-time alerts and notifications to keep the care team informed of critical events. For example, caregivers can receive alerts about a patient's fall, change in vital signs, or missed medications. Healthcare professionals can be promptly notified of any emergent situations, allowing for rapid response and intervention.

❖ Shared Care Plans: Collaborative care models utilize shared care plans that outline the patient's treatment goals and care strategies. These plans are accessible to all care team members, allowing everyone to be on the same page regarding the patient's care journey. Shared care plans foster teamwork and ensure that all interventions align with the patient's needs and preferences.

❖ Remote Monitoring Integration: Remote monitoring devices can be integrated with collaborative care models to provide real-time health data to healthcare professionals and caregivers. Vital signs, activity levels, and medication adherence data collected by these devices can be shared with the care team, enabling proactive management of the patient's health.

❖ Secure Data Sharing: Secure data sharing platforms allow caregivers and healthcare professionals to share patient information while maintaining strict privacy and security measures. Encryption and secure data storage ensure that sensitive information remains confidential and compliant with privacy regulations.

❖ Care Transitions Support: Technology supports smooth care transitions when patients move between different care settings, such as hospitals, nursing homes, and home care. With shared access to patient records and communication tools, the care team can ensure a seamless transfer of information and coordinated care during these transitions.

Collaborative care models empowered by technology foster a patient-centric approach to healthcare, where all stakeholders work together to optimize patient outcomes and experiences. By leveraging technology to bridge communication gaps and share vital information, caregivers and healthcare professionals can provide coordinated, efficient, and compassionate care to aging individuals and individuals with disabilities.

In "Tech and Aging: Enhancing Lives Through Assistive Technologies," we emphasize the importance of collaborative care models with technology. Through real-life case studies and expert insights, we demonstrate how technology promotes collaboration, enhances care coordination, and fosters a patient-centered healthcare ecosystem.

CHAPTER IX
Policy, Regulations, and Funding for Assistive Technologies

A. Government Initiatives and Support

Government initiatives and support play a vital role in fostering the development, accessibility, and affordability of assistive technologies. Recognizing the importance of these technologies in enhancing the lives of aging individuals and people with disabilities, governments around the world have implemented policies and regulations to promote their adoption and integration into various sectors. These initiatives span from research and development funding to regulatory frameworks that ensure safety and efficacy.

❖ Research and Development Grants: Government agencies often allocate grants and funding to support research and development in the field of assistive technologies. These grants encourage innovators, researchers, and technology companies to invest in creating cutting-edge solutions that address the unique needs of the aging population and individuals with disabilities. The financial support stimulates the advancement of assistive technologies, leading to more effective and accessible solutions.

❖ Assistive Technology Accessibility Standards: To promote the widespread adoption of assistive technologies, governments establish accessibility standards and guidelines. These standards ensure that technology developers consider the needs of users with diverse abilities during the design and development phases. By adhering to these standards, technology manufacturers create products that are more inclusive and user-friendly for individuals with disabilities.

❖ Inclusive Education and Employment Initiatives: Governments emphasize inclusive education and employment initiatives that support individuals with disabilities in accessing education and entering the workforce. Assistive technologies play a crucial role in these initiatives, as they empower individuals to overcome barriers and participate more fully in educational and professional settings. Government support in funding assistive technologies for educational and workplace environments enhances opportunities for equal participation and success.

❖ Health Insurance Coverage: Many governments work to ensure that health insurance policies cover the cost of essential assistive technologies. By including these technologies in insurance coverage, the financial burden on individuals and their families is reduced, making them more accessible to those who need them. Health insurance support contributes to better health outcomes and improved quality of life for individuals utilizing assistive technologies.

❖ Public Awareness and Education Campaigns: Governments often conduct public awareness and education campaigns to promote the benefits of assistive technologies and reduce stigma. These campaigns aim to increase understanding and acceptance of assistive solutions, encouraging individuals to seek appropriate technologies that can improve their lives. Public awareness initiatives foster a more inclusive society and promote the integration of assistive technologies into mainstream culture.

❖ Accessibility in Public Spaces: Governments advocate for accessibility in public spaces, ensuring that buildings, transportation systems, and public facilities are designed to accommodate individuals with disabilities. This commitment to universal design promotes the use of assistive technologies and creates an environment that is more inclusive and welcoming to all members of society.

❖ Support for Caregivers: Recognizing the significant role of caregivers in the care of aging individuals and individuals with disabilities, governments provide support and resources for caregivers. This includes funding for respite care, training programs, and access to technology that can assist caregivers in their daily tasks. By supporting caregivers, governments strengthen the overall caregiving ecosystem and improve the well-being of both caregivers and care recipients.

Government initiatives and support are essential in driving the advancement and accessibility of assistive technologies. These efforts not only improve the quality of life for aging individuals and people with disabilities but also promote inclusion, equity, and societal well-being. By continuing to invest in policies, regulations, and funding, governments can create an environment where assistive technologies thrive, empowering individuals to live with dignity and independence.

In "Tech and Aging: Enhancing Lives Through Assistive Technologies," we explore the impact of government initiatives and support on the field of assistive technologies. Through real-life examples and expert perspectives, we illustrate how governments play a crucial role in shaping the future of assistive technologies and fostering a more inclusive society.

B. Private Sector Investment and Innovations

The private sector plays a significant role in driving innovation, accessibility, and affordability in the realm of assistive technologies. Through private sector investment and entrepreneurial endeavors, a diverse array of assistive solutions has emerged, catering to the diverse needs of aging individuals and people with disabilities. These innovations leverage cutting-edge technologies and creative approaches to improve the lives of individuals with diverse abilities.

❖ Venture Capital Funding: Private sector investment, including venture capital funding, has fueled the development and commercialization of groundbreaking assistive technologies. Venture capital firms recognize the potential of assistive solutions and provide financial support to startups and established companies working on innovative products and services. This funding allows innovators to bring their ideas to fruition and accelerate the pace of technological advancements.

❖ Startups and Entrepreneurship: The dynamic landscape of assistive technologies attracts entrepreneurs and startups eager to make a positive impact on the lives of individuals with disabilities. Startups often embrace agile and disruptive approaches to develop unique assistive solutions that address specific challenges faced by their target audience. Their entrepreneurial spirit fosters a culture of innovation and creativity, resulting in novel and effective products.

❖ Tech Companies and Corporate Social Responsibility: Leading technology companies recognize the importance of corporate social responsibility and invest in assistive technologies as part of their initiatives. These companies leverage their technical expertise, research capabilities, and global reach to create assistive solutions with a broad impact. Tech giants often collaborate with nonprofits and organizations to design and distribute technologies that address pressing societal needs.

❖ Gamification and User Engagement: Private sector investment has driven the integration of gamification elements in assistive technologies, making them more engaging and enjoyable for users. Gamified apps and platforms motivate individuals to participate actively in therapy exercises, cognitive training, and other rehabilitative activities. Gamification enhances user motivation and adherence to treatment plans, leading to better outcomes.

❖ Connected Devices and IoT: The Internet of Things (IoT) has revolutionized the world of assistive technologies. Connected devices and wearables provide real-time data and feedback, allowing for remote monitoring and personalized interventions. IoT-enabled assistive technologies offer a seamless and integrated user experience, empowering individuals to manage their health and well-being proactively.

❖ 3D Printing and Customization: Private sector innovations have led to the adoption of 3D printing in the development of assistive devices. 3D printing technology enables the customization of devices, ensuring a perfect fit and addressing individual needs. This cost-effective and rapid manufacturing process has democratized access to assistive devices, making them more accessible to diverse populations.

❖ Mobile Apps and Accessibility Features: Mobile apps have become powerful tools in the world of assistive technologies. Private sector developers create mobile apps that cater to specific disabilities, such as apps for communication, navigation, and sensory assistance. Accessibility features on smartphones, including voice recognition and screen readers, further enhance usability for individuals with disabilities.

❖ Robotics and AI Integration: Private sector investment has facilitated the integration of robotics and artificial intelligence (AI) in assistive technologies. AI-driven robotics offer personalized support, while AI algorithms enhance the intelligence and responsiveness of assistive devices. Robotics and AI enable a higher degree of autonomy and independence for users, revolutionizing caregiving and support for aging individuals.

The private sector's commitment to assistive technologies has resulted in a dynamic and innovative ecosystem, driving forward progress in the field. Private sector investment and entrepreneurial ventures bring fresh perspectives and creativity, leading to transformative solutions that enhance the lives of aging individuals and individuals with disabilities.

In "Tech and Aging: Enhancing Lives Through Assistive Technologies," we explore the impact of private sector investment and innovations. Through real-life case studies and expert insights, we showcase how the private sector's dedication to assistive technologies fosters inclusive and empowering solutions, shaping a future where technology enriches the lives of individuals of all abilities.

C. Legal and Ethical Considerations

As the field of assistive technologies continues to advance, it is essential to address the legal and ethical implications surrounding their development, deployment, and usage. While these technologies offer immense benefits to aging individuals and people with disabilities, careful consideration of privacy, safety, and equitable access is crucial to ensure that they are deployed responsibly and ethically.

- ❖ Data Privacy and Security: Assistive technologies often collect and process sensitive personal data to provide personalized support and services. Ensuring robust data privacy and security measures is paramount to protect the confidentiality and integrity of this information. Developers and service providers must comply with relevant data protection regulations and adopt encryption, access controls, and secure data storage to safeguard user data.

- ❖ Informed Consent: Users of assistive technologies, especially those relying on AI and data analysis, should provide informed consent for the collection and use of their data. Transparent communication about data usage, potential risks, and the benefits of the technology is necessary to obtain meaningful consent from users. Ethical considerations demand that users have the right to understand and control how their data is used.

❖ Accessibility and Inclusivity: Legal and ethical considerations underscore the importance of ensuring that assistive technologies are accessible and inclusive for individuals with diverse abilities. Regulatory frameworks and accessibility standards should be in place to guide the design and development of technologies that are usable by everyone, regardless of their physical or cognitive abilities.

❖ Equity in Access: Governments and policymakers need to address the issue of equity in access to assistive technologies. Financial barriers should not limit access to these vital resources for vulnerable populations. Funding and support should be available to ensure that individuals with disabilities, regardless of their socioeconomic status, can access the assistive technologies that meet their needs.

❖ Bias and Fairness: AI-driven assistive technologies should be developed with attention to fairness and bias mitigation. AI algorithms should be carefully designed and regularly audited to avoid perpetuating existing biases in their decision-making processes. The goal is to ensure that the technology operates in a fair and equitable manner, free from discrimination.

❖ Liability and Responsibility: Legal considerations arise concerning liability and responsibility when assistive technologies are integrated into healthcare settings or used for critical tasks. Clear guidelines should be in place to allocate responsibility between the technology provider, the caregiver, and the user in case of adverse events or failures. Ethical concerns emphasize the need to ensure that technology is used responsibly, with the well-being of users as the top priority.

❖ Human-Machine Interaction: The legal and ethical dimensions of human-machine interaction should be carefully examined. For example, in the case of robotic companions or caregiving devices, it is essential to set boundaries for appropriate interactions and clarify the role of the machine versus the role of the human caregiver.

❖ Transparency and Explainability: The legal and ethical implications of AI-driven assistive technologies necessitate transparency and explainability in their decision-making processes. Users and caregivers should have insights into how the technology arrived at specific recommendations or actions to foster trust and confidence in the technology's use.

Addressing these legal and ethical considerations is crucial to ensure that assistive technologies are developed, deployed, and used responsibly. By aligning policies, regulations, and funding with ethical principles, society can harness the full potential of these technologies to empower aging individuals and individuals with disabilities, while safeguarding their rights, privacy, and dignity.

In "Tech and Aging: Enhancing Lives Through Assistive Technologies," we explore the legal and ethical landscape surrounding assistive technologies. Through expert analysis and real-world examples, we demonstrate the importance of striking a balance between innovation and ethical responsibility, ultimately shaping a future where technology fosters a more inclusive and compassionate society.

CHAPTER X
Future Prospects: The Road Ahead

A. Predictions and Forecasts for Tech and Aging

The intersection of technology and aging is a dynamic and ever-evolving field, with exciting possibilities for the future. As technology continues to advance at a rapid pace, it is anticipated that the landscape of assistive technologies will undergo significant transformations, providing even greater benefits to aging individuals and people with disabilities. Several key predictions and forecasts shed light on the road ahead for tech and aging.

❖ AI-Powered Personalized Solutions: Artificial Intelligence (AI) will play a central role in the development of personalized assistive technologies. AI algorithms will gain a deeper understanding of individual preferences, abilities, and needs, enabling the creation of highly tailored solutions. These technologies will adapt and evolve in real-time, ensuring optimal support for each user's unique requirements.

❖ Seamless Integration of IoT and Wearables: The Internet of Things (IoT) will seamlessly integrate with assistive technologies, making them more interconnected and efficient. Wearables equipped with sensors will provide continuous health monitoring and activity tracking, allowing caregivers and healthcare professionals to monitor well-being remotely. IoT-enabled devices will foster proactive interventions and personalized care plans.

❖ Virtual and Augmented Reality Advancements: Virtual Reality (VR) and Augmented Reality (AR) will continue to transform the landscape of assistive technologies. VR will offer immersive training and rehabilitation experiences, while AR will provide real-time assistance and visual aids for daily tasks. Advancements in VR and AR will enhance social interaction, therapy, and educational experiences for aging individuals and individuals with disabilities.

❖ Greater Accessibility and Inclusivity: The push for greater accessibility and inclusivity will drive the development of more user-friendly and universally designed assistive technologies. Innovations will focus on addressing a wide range of disabilities and challenges, ensuring that aging individuals and people with diverse abilities can benefit from these technologies without barriers.

❖ Robotics for Enhanced Care: Robotic technologies will become more prevalent in caregiving and assistance roles. Social robots will provide companionship and emotional support, reducing feelings of loneliness and isolation among aging individuals. Robots will also assist with tasks like medication reminders, home maintenance, and mobility support.

❖ AI-Driven Predictive Healthcare: AI-driven predictive healthcare models will enable early identification and intervention for health conditions in aging individuals. By analyzing data from remote monitoring devices and health records, AI algorithms will predict health risks and recommend preventive measures, improving overall health outcomes.

❖ Ethical AI and Responsible Deployment: As AI becomes more pervasive in assistive technologies, the focus on ethical considerations and responsible deployment will intensify. Governments, organizations, and developers will collaborate to establish clear guidelines and regulations for AI applications in the field, ensuring that these technologies align with ethical principles and respect individual rights.

❖ Global Collaboration and Partnerships: The future of tech and aging will witness increased global collaboration and partnerships between governments, private sector entities, nonprofit organizations, and research institutions. Collective efforts will drive the development of innovative solutions and promote the equitable distribution of assistive technologies worldwide.

In conclusion, the future of tech and aging holds immense promise, driven by cutting-edge innovations and a commitment to inclusivity. Predictions and forecasts paint a compelling picture of an interconnected ecosystem of personalized and AI-driven technologies that empower aging individuals and individuals with disabilities to lead fulfilling and independent lives. As society embraces these advancements, it becomes ever more essential to foster ethical considerations, privacy protections, and equitable access to ensure that technology continues to enhance lives and create a more inclusive world.

In "Tech and Aging: Enhancing Lives Through Assistive Technologies," we explore the exciting prospects for tech and aging, showcasing how the future of assistive technologies will transform the lives of individuals of all ages and abilities. Through expert insights and visionary forecasts, we aim to inspire a future where technology becomes a powerful enabler, enriching the human experience and promoting dignity and well-being for all.

B. Challenges and Opportunities for the Future

As we embark on the future of tech and aging, several challenges and opportunities await us in the development, deployment, and adoption of assistive technologies. While these innovations hold great potential to enhance the lives of aging individuals and people with disabilities, addressing the following challenges will be crucial to maximizing their impact and creating a more inclusive society.

Challenges:

- ❖ Affordability and Accessibility: One of the significant challenges is ensuring that assistive technologies remain affordable and accessible to all individuals who need them. While technology advancements often come with initial high costs, it is essential to find ways to make these solutions more financially attainable for individuals with diverse socioeconomic backgrounds.

- ❖ Technology Literacy and Digital Divide: The digital divide remains a barrier for many aging individuals, especially those from underserved communities. Bridging the technology literacy gap is essential to ensure that older adults can fully benefit from assistive technologies. Comprehensive training and support programs will be necessary to empower older adults to navigate and utilize these technologies effectively.

❖ User-Centered Design: To be truly effective, assistive technologies must be designed with a deep understanding of the needs, preferences, and abilities of the end-users. User-centered design is critical to creating solutions that are intuitive, user-friendly, and tailored to the unique requirements of each individual.

❖ Data Privacy and Security: As assistive technologies collect and analyze sensitive personal data, ensuring robust data privacy and security is paramount. Striking a balance between data collection for personalized support and safeguarding user privacy will be a significant challenge that requires ongoing attention and regulatory guidance.

❖ Bias in AI Algorithms: AI-driven assistive technologies rely on algorithms that may inadvertently inherit biases present in training data.

Ethical considerations demand a vigilant approach to identify and address bias in AI algorithms to ensure fair and equitable outcomes for all users.

Opportunities:

* Collaborative Innovation: The future presents exciting opportunities for collaborative innovation. Governments, private sector entities, academia, and nonprofit organizations can join forces to pool resources and expertise, driving the development of innovative solutions that address complex challenges in aging and disability support.

* Holistic Health and Well-Being: Assistive technologies have the potential to support holistic health and well-being by integrating physical, cognitive, and emotional aspects of individuals' lives. Technologies that provide personalized health insights and promote self-care will empower individuals to take an active role in managing their overall well-being.

❖ Global Market Expansion: As the global population continues to age, there is a vast market for assistive technologies worldwide. By investing in research, development, and distribution on a global scale, innovators can tap into this market potential and improve the lives of millions of aging individuals and individuals with disabilities.

❖ Advancements in AI and Robotics: Advancements in AI and robotics open doors to more sophisticated and context-aware assistive technologies. These technologies can adapt to users' changing needs and provide more intelligent and empathetic support.

❖ Inclusive Smart Cities: Smart city initiatives can embrace assistive technologies to create more inclusive urban environments. By incorporating accessibility features, IoT-enabled devices, and user-friendly interfaces, cities can cater to the needs of aging populations and individuals with disabilities.

As we navigate the challenges and seize the opportunities in the future of tech and aging, a collaborative and inclusive approach will be instrumental in shaping a world where technology enhances lives and promotes social inclusion. Embracing ethical considerations, data privacy, and user-centered design will be essential to harness the full potential of assistive technologies while ensuring that they prioritize the well-being and dignity of their users.

In "Tech and Aging: Enhancing Lives Through Assistive Technologies," we explore the challenges and opportunities that lie ahead. Through expert insights and real-world examples, we aim to inspire a future where technology and compassion intersect, fostering a world where aging individuals and individuals with disabilities can thrive and live life to the fullest.

C. Importance of Continuous Research and Development

Continuous research and development (R&D) in the field of assistive technologies are paramount to unlock the full potential of these innovations and address the evolving needs of aging individuals and people with disabilities. The journey to an inclusive and empowering future requires a steadfast commitment to advancing technology and pushing the boundaries of what is possible. The importance of continuous R&D in the realm of tech and aging cannot be overstated, and it encompasses several key aspects.

❖ Innovation and Advancements: R&D serves as the engine of innovation, driving the creation of new and improved assistive technologies. With each breakthrough, we witness advancements that enhance functionality, usability, and effectiveness. Through innovation, we can develop cutting-edge solutions that revolutionize the way we support and care for aging populations.

❖ User-Centric Approach: Continuous R&D enables a user-centric approach, placing the needs and preferences of aging individuals and individuals with disabilities at the forefront. By actively seeking feedback from users and incorporating their insights into the development process, R&D teams can create technologies that truly resonate with the end-users and address their unique challenges.

❖ Personalization and Tailoring: As R&D progresses, we move closer to a future where assistive technologies are highly personalized and tailored to individual requirements. Personalization ensures that the technology adapts to the changing needs of users, providing relevant support and services that evolve with them over time.

❖ Addressing Complex Challenges: The challenges faced by aging individuals and individuals with disabilities are multifaceted and continually evolving. Continuous R&D enables us to tackle these challenges head-on, developing solutions that address physical, cognitive, and emotional needs in a comprehensive and integrated manner.

❖ Integration of Emerging Technologies: With technology constantly evolving, continuous R&D allows for the seamless integration of emerging technologies into assistive solutions. From AI and IoT to robotics and virtual reality, integrating cutting-edge technologies empowers assistive devices to perform more intelligently and efficiently.

❖ Bridging Gaps and Reducing Barriers: R&D efforts are instrumental in identifying and bridging gaps in the current landscape of assistive technologies. Whether it is affordability, accessibility, or usability, continuous R&D aims to reduce barriers and ensure that these technologies are widely available to those who can benefit from them.

❖ Evidence-Based Practice: R&D promotes evidence-based practice by providing scientific data and insights that demonstrate the efficacy and impact of assistive technologies. Through rigorous research, we can build a solid foundation of evidence, gaining a deeper understanding of how these technologies improve the lives of their users.

❖ Collaboration and Knowledge Sharing: Continuous R&D fosters collaboration among researchers, developers, healthcare professionals, and caregivers. Knowledge sharing and interdisciplinary cooperation lead to a more comprehensive understanding of aging and disability support, enabling cross-pollination of ideas and expertise.

❖ Anticipating Future Needs: By continuously investing in R&D, we can anticipate future needs and challenges associated with aging and disability support. Proactively developing technologies that address potential issues helps us stay ahead of the curve and remain agile in adapting to changing circumstances.

In "Tech and Aging: Enhancing Lives Through Assistive Technologies," we underscore the importance of continuous research and development in shaping the future of tech and aging. Through real-life case studies and expert insights, we highlight the transformative impact of R&D efforts, inspiring a collective commitment to innovation and a future where assistive technologies empower and enrich the lives of aging individuals and individuals with disabilities.

Conclusion

A. Recapitulation of Key Points

"Tech and Aging: Enhancing Lives Through Assistive Technologies" delves into the transformative intersection of technology and aging, highlighting the profound impact of assistive technologies on the lives of aging individuals and people with disabilities. Throughout the book, we have explored various aspects of this dynamic field, from understanding the challenges of aging to envisioning a future filled with innovative solutions that promote inclusivity and independence. Let us recapitulate the key points covered in this enlightening journey.

❖ The Intersection of Technology and Aging: We began by exploring the intersection of technology and aging, where assistive technologies play a pivotal role in empowering aging individuals and individuals with disabilities to lead fulfilling lives. The merging of technology and compassion offers boundless opportunities for enhancing well-being and independence.

❖ Importance of Assistive Technologies: We emphasized the significance of assistive technologies in addressing the unique challenges faced by aging individuals and individuals with disabilities. These technologies bridge the gap between abilities and limitations, fostering autonomy and improving quality of life.

❖ Overview of the Book's Scope: The book's scope encompassed a comprehensive understanding of aging and its challenges, the evolution of assistive technologies, and their diverse applications in mobility, cognition, communication, and health monitoring. Additionally, we explored the barriers and opportunities in integrating technology into the caregiving landscape.

❖ Demographic Trends and Aging Population: We delved into demographic trends, highlighting the global aging population and its implications on healthcare, social services, and caregiving. As the population ages, the demand for innovative assistive technologies grows, making it imperative to address the unique needs of older adults.

❖ Physical and Cognitive Changes in Aging: Understanding the physical and cognitive changes that accompany aging was crucial in designing effective assistive solutions. We explored how technologies can support mobility, memory, cognition, and sensory abilities, empowering individuals to overcome age-related challenges.

❖ Social and Emotional Impact of Aging: We recognized the importance of addressing the social and emotional impact of aging, particularly the effects of isolation and loneliness. Assistive technologies offer solutions to foster social connections, improve mental health, and enhance emotional well-being.

❖ Historical Overview of Assistive Devices: To appreciate the evolution of assistive technologies, we explored their historical development, from simple devices to the sophisticated solutions of today. This historical context showcases the progress and innovation achieved over time.

❖ Technological Advancements in Recent Years: Recent technological advancements, particularly in AI, IoT, robotics, and virtual reality, have revolutionized the capabilities of assistive technologies. These innovations drive personalized and context-aware solutions that cater to individual needs.

❖ Current State of Assistive Technologies: We examined the current state of assistive technologies, highlighting the range of devices and services available to support aging individuals and individuals with disabilities. The diversity of offerings showcases the breadth and depth of the assistive technology landscape.

❖ Types of Assistive Technologies: In-depth explorations of mobility assistance devices, cognitive support technologies, sensory aids, communication tools, and health monitoring solutions showcased the versatility of assistive technologies in meeting diverse needs.

❖ Addressing Barriers and Ethical Concerns: We recognized the challenges of integrating technology into caregiving, emphasizing the importance of accessibility, user-centered design, privacy, and ethical considerations in creating responsible and compassionate solutions.

❖ Case Studies: Real-Life Impact: Real-life case studies brought to light the transformative impact of assistive technologies on individuals' lives. Personal testimonials and success stories demonstrated the positive outcomes these technologies bring to users and their caregivers.

❖ Emerging Trends: The exploration of emerging trends in AI, robotics, and virtual reality underscored the exciting prospects for the future of assistive technologies. These trends hold the potential to revolutionize caregiving and support for aging populations.